Essential
AROMATHERAPY

p

Essential
AROMATHERAPY

Edited by
JENNY PLUCKNETT

WARNING

If you have a medical condition, or are pregnant, the information in this book
should not be followed without consulting your doctor first.
All guidelines, warnings and instructions should be read carefully
before embarking on any of the treatments.
The publisher cannot accept responsibility for injuries or damage
arising out of a failure to comply with the above.

This is a Parragon Book
This edition published in 2001

Parragon
Queen Street House
4 Queen Street
Bath BA1 1HE, UK

ISBN 0-75256-364-5

Printed in Italy

Produced by Kingfisher Design, London

Series Editor Jenny Plucknett
Series Design Pedro Prá-Lopez, Kingfisher Design, London

Aromatherapy consultant Alison J Wilkinson BABTAC IFA reg. Dip.
Editing Margaret Crowther
Illustrations Jill Moore
Plant illustrations pages 11, 13, 15, 17, 19 Wayne Ford
Typesetting/DTP Frances Prá-Lopez, Kingfisher Design, London

Contents

What is Aromatherapy?

WHEN WERE PLANT OILS FIRST USED?

The Egyptians were the first to distil plants in order to extract their essential oils. They used them medicinally, in religious ceremonies, as beautifying skin and face potions and perfumes.

WHY ARE THESE OILS STILL USED TODAY?

Although aromatherapy is based on more than 6000 years' knowledge, the term was first used only 65 years ago. A French chemist named Gattefossé owned a perfumery business. One day he burnt his hand, plunged it into a vat of Lavender oil and found the burn healed quickly. This began a lifelong interest in studying the therapeutic properties of plant oils. Recently biochemists have isolated dozens of ingredients in essential oils that account for the amazing properties they have.

WHAT IS AN ESSENTIAL OIL?

Essential oils all come from plants and the liquid is held in tiny
sacs somewhere on the plant. It may be taken from the petals,
roots, rind, stalk, seeds, sap, nuts, leaves or the bark.
It is important to obtain essential oils from a reputable source.
It is now possible to buy fine oils from specialist beauty outlets,
mail order companies, health food shops and many drug stores.
Your nearest aromatherapy association will offer guidance.

WHERE CAN I USE AROMATHERAPY OILS?

Apart from using the oils in massage, the most widely known
method, oils can become a major ingredient in beauty
treatments, can be added to baths as a restorative, or used in the
home to add aroma, to clean surfaces or even repel insects!
But, before you start to use essential oils, please make sure
you read pages 8-9, Using oils safely.

Using Oils Safely

Using essential oils is a pleasurable experience, stimulating your sense of smell, your moods, behaviour and mental and physical well being. Follow these basic rules to ensure that you use the oils properly and enjoy the event without any problems to yourself or anyone else.

❋ Essential oils are potent. Only ever measure them out in drops.

❋ Never apply undiluted essential oils to the skin (*see right*).

❋ Never take essential oils internally.

❋ Never increase the dose of essential oil. Some oils are toxic in large amounts.

❋ Apply essential oils only as instructed for treating common ailments. If symptoms persist seek medical advice.

❋ Always keep essential oils out of reach of children.

❋ Treat a splash of oil in the eye by rinsing it out with a few drops of pure, Sweet Almond oil, not water. Seek medical advice.

❋ Don't shower or bath preferably for 24 hours (12 hours if this is not possible) after an aromatherapy massage. Oils take that long to fully penetrate the skin.

❋ Don't pour the blended oil straight from a glass bottle when massaging. Hands become slippery and the bottle could slip and break. Instead use a bowl and dip your hands into it or put the mixture temporarily into a plastic bottle with a squirting top.

❋ Don't store essential oils, pure or diluted, in plastic containers. They could become contaminated.

WARNING

DILUTE OILS BEFORE USE

Dilute all essential oils in either water or a carrier oil before use, except where specifically instructed otherwise. See pages 22-23 for more information.

OILS TO SPECIALLY AVOID DURING PREGNANCY

If you are pregnant the information in this book should not be followed without consulting your doctor first.

ANGELICA • BASIL • CEDARWOOD • CITRONELLA • FENNEL • JUNIPER • LAUREL
MARJORAM • MYRRH • ROSEMARY • SAGE • TARRAGON • THYME • YARROW

OILS THAT ARE PHOTO-TOXIC

These oils can irritate skin, especially if it is exposed to sunshine after application. Use half the drops recommended for other oils (less than one third the drops of lemon) and do not go into the sun for at least six hours after application.

ANGELICA • BERGAMOT • CITRONELLA • GINGER • LEMON • LIME
MANDARIN • ORANGE • (BASIL and LAUREL can also irritate skin)

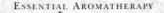

— 1 —
Lavender

LAVANDULA AUGUSTIFOLIA

Probably the most useful, versatile and popular
essential oil, Lavender was a favourite bathtime cleanser
with the Romans. It is native to the Mediterranean region
and cultivated in many countries in Europe, most
particularly France, Italy and the United Kingdom.

HOW LAVENDER OIL WORKS

Depending on how it is used, and the other oils with which
it is mixed, Lavender can be either stimulating or relaxing. It is
also a powerful antiseptic and healer. Excellent for tension,
tiredness and depression, Lavender calms, refreshes, invigorates
and lifts the spirits. A very safe essential oil, it can be
used in many ways, including for massage,
baths and inhalations.

WHAT LAVENDER OIL MIXES WITH

The addition of a second oil can sometimes improve an oil's therapeutic properties. For instance, the anti-inflammatory action of Chamomile is strengthened by the addition of Lavender.

Lavender mixes with almost all the other essential oils. However, in all cases it is best not to mix more than three essential oils together. The best rule is to keep mixes simple. Lavender goes particularly well with the other floral oils: Geranium, Jasmine, Mimosa, Neroli, Rose, Violet and Ylang-ylang.

Rapid Remedies using Lavender Oil

❋ Add 8-10 drops Lavender oil to a hot bath to relieve anxiety and make you feel pleasantly drowsy.

❋ In a cool bath use 4 drops Lavender mixed with 4 drops Thyme and 2 drops Peppermint to refresh and energize.

❋ Add 5 drops Lavender oil to 1 litre (2 pints/5 cups) boiling water in a bowl and inhale this to clear the head and lift the spirits.

Lemon

CITRUS LIMON

Cleansing and invigorating, Lemon oil was used by the ancient Romans to counteract stomach upsets and to sweeten the breath. The British Navy once used it to prevent scurvy. The oil is extracted from the fresh rind of the fruit and lemons are grown for this purpose in Spain, Florida, Portugal, Italy, Israel and California.

HOW LEMON OIL WORKS

Lemon oil, with its tangy, fresh citrus smell, is stimulating, invigorating and astringent. It is also deodorizing, diuretic and antiseptic. Lemon is used for clearing the head during a cold or when you are mentally exhausted. It provides energy for an aching body and boosts circulation, warming hands and feet. Lemon can also be used for treating cellulite. Use Lemon oil for massage, baths and inhalations.

WHAT LEMON OIL MIXES WITH

Lemon oil mixes with almost all the widely used essential oils. However do not use it with other citrus oils or Angelica, Camphor, Galbanum, Ginger, Mimosa, Tarragon, Valerian, Violet and Yarrow.

Rapid remedies using Lemon oil

❋ Inhale 2 drops of Lemon oil from a tissue placed on the pillow or in a breastpocket to relieve the symptoms of a cold.

❋ On a cold night boost your circulation with up to 3 drops (2 drops for a sensitive skin) in a hot bath.

❋ Add 2-3 drops to a cleaning cloth to wipe over surfaces and act as a deodorizer in the home.

WARNING

Lemon oil can cause skin irritation unless thoroughly diluted. Use only small quantities, less than one third the quantity recommended for other oils. Do not expose the skin to sunshine for at least six hours after application.

Eucalyptus

EUCALYPTUS GLOBULUS

The distinctive smell of Eucalyptus oil is easily recognized.
It was a favourite medicinal herb with native Australians, the Aborigines,
who crushed the leaves to heal wounds, fight infection and relieve
muscular pain. The wood was also used on cooking fires to add
flavour to food. The oil is extracted from the twigs and leaves of the
Blue Gum tree. A native of Australia, the tree is now grown
commercially in California, Spain and Portugal.

HOW EUCALYPTUS OIL WORKS

The oil is stimulating and has been used in cough and cold remedies for
decades. A powerful antiseptic, it kills airborne germs and has a
cooling effect on the skin. It is an excellent decongestant
for fever, flu, coughs, colds or sinusitis.
It soothes muscular aches, sprains and pains and helps
to heal abrasions. Use Eucalyptus oil in massage,
baths and inhalations.

WHAT EUCALYPTUS OIL MIXES WITH

Eucalyptus oil can be mixed with about half of the most widely used essential oils including Angelica, Basil, Bay, Atlas Cedarwood, Chamomile, Frankincense, Geranium, Ginger, Juniper, Laurel, Lavender, Lemon, Marjoram, Peppermint, Pine, Rosemary, Clary Sage, Sandalwood, Spruce, Tea Tree and Thyme.

Rapid remedies using Eucalyptus oil

❋ Place a few drops in a dish of hot water over a radiator to disinfect a room.

❋ Add 5 drops to a hot bath to relieve congestion during a cough or cold.

❋ Dilute with carrier oil (*see page 22-23*) and massage into aching muscles.

Jasmine

JASMINUM OFFICINALE

Prized, above all, for its romantic, rich, exotic scent Jasmine makes almost everyone who smells it feel better. Jasmine is the special ingredient in most of the great, classic perfumes, adding a distinctive, sensual appeal. It takes eight million flowers, all hand picked before dawn, to extract just one kilogram of oil and this makes Jasmine one of the most expensive essential oils. It is grown in France, Egypt, Morocco, India and Italy.

HOW JASMINE OIL WORKS

The oil is deep red in colour and smells as fragrant as the tiny white star-shaped flowers it comes from. Jasmine oil is uplifting and relaxing, leaving the recipient confident, optimistic and slightly euphoric. It is good for dry or sensitive skins and for aches and cramps. Jasmine oil can be used in massage, for baths and inhalations. Use it to treat depression, stress, fatigue, irritability or apathy. It is also good for PMT and is an excellent skin softener.

WHAT JASMINE OIL MIXES WITH

Mix with Bergamot, Atlas Cedarwood, Chamomile, Geranium, Ginger, Lavender, Lemon, Lemongrass, Mimosa, Patchouli, Rose, Rosewood, Clary Sage, Sandalwood, and Ylang-ylang.

Rapid remedies using Jasmine oil

❋ Add 8 drops Jasmine oil to a bath to counteract stress or fatigue.

❋ Place up to 8 drops in a vaporizer, or add 12 drops to the wood for a fire before you light it. This will scent the room and create a mellow atmosphere for a dinner party.

❋ Add 2 drops Jasmine oil to a basin of warm water for a final face rinse after cleansing. Leave to dry naturally to help to soften the skin.

Sandalwood

SANTALUM ALBUM

A rich, fruity-sweet, woody smell has made Sandalwood a favourite perfume ingredient since early times. Sandalwood was used by the ancient Egyptians, Chinese and Indians for incense and embalming. Medicinally it was used to cure skin inflammations and to help discharge mucus. Oil is extracted from the roots and heart wood of the tree. Most oil comes from India but the tree is also cultivated in Malaysia, Sri Lanka and Indonesia.

HOW SANDALWOOD OIL WORKS

The oil is relaxing and is regarded as a sedative and an aphrodisiac. It is also astringent and antiseptic. In aromatherapy it is used for insomnia, tension, stress, depression, and cracked or chapped skin. It is also a good cough or cold expectorant.

WHAT SANDALWOOD OIL MIXES WITH

Sandalwood oil can be mixed with a wide range of other essential oils.
Some of the most popular are Bay, Bergamot, Chamomile,
Eucalyptus, Frankincense, Geranium, Jasmine, Juniper,
Lavender, Lemon, Marjoram, Mimosa, Myrrh, Neroli,
Patchouli, Peppermint, Rose, Rosemary,
Tea Tree and Ylang-ylang.

Rapid remedies using Sandalwood oil

❉ Place 3 drops Sandalwood with 3 drops Ylang-ylang and
2 drops Pine in a hot bath on a cold winter day
for a soothing, sensual soak.

❉ For callouses or rough skin massage feet with
3 drops Lavender and 3 drops Sandalwood
in 30ml (1fl oz/6 tsp) olive oil.

❉ Inhale 5 drops Sandalwood in 1 litre (2 pints)
boiling water to clear congestion.

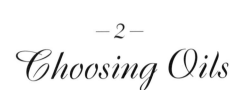

— 2 —

Choosing Oils

From such a wide range of essential oils it can be difficult to make an initial choice. As well as scent, you need to bear in mind those oils you will want to use for massage and beauty preparations plus those that will be most useful for their therapeutic properties. Make a list of about ten oils which you think will best fulfil your individual needs then check the aromas you prefer in the shop before buying.

POINTS TO CONSIDER WHEN MAKING YOUR LIST

❋ **Good mixers** Those oils that mix well with a wide range of other oils are particularly useful. See pages 24-25 for more information.

❋ **Therapeutic properties** Look through the A-Z on pages 52-62 for those that have the broadest range of therapeutic uses.

* **Beauty preparations** Check the oils recommended for beauty preparations, for baths and for home use on pages 28-37. Decide on the applications that you are most likely to follow.

* **Essential oil scents** Oils fall into one of five groups: floral, green, spicy, citrus, woody/balsamic. Choose oils from the groups which contain the aromas you prefer.

ESSENTIAL OIL GROUPS

Floral	Green	Spicy	Citrus	Woody/Balsamic
Geranium	Basil	Camphor	Bergamot	Ambrette
Jasmine	Chamomile	Fennel	Citronella	Angelica
Lavender	Clary Sage	Ginger	Lemon	Cedarwood
Mimosa	Eucalyptus	Juniper	Lemongrass	Frankincense
Neroli	Galbanum	Laurel	Lime	Marigold
Rose	Peppermint	Marjoram	Mandarin	Patchouli
Violet	Pine	Myrrh	Orange	Rosewood
Ylang-ylang	Rosemary	Tarragon	Petitgrain	Sandalwood
	Spruce	Tea Tree		Valerian
	Thyme			Yarrow

IDEAL SMALL COLLECTION

The five oils covered in Chapter 1: LAVENDER • LEMON • EUCALYPTUS JASMINE • SANDALWOOD
plus any of the following: CHAMOMILE • GERANIUM • NEROLI • PATCHOULI PEPPERMINT • ROSE • YLANG-YLANG

Diluting Oils

Essential oils are potent and are, almost always, only used diluted. Never increase the quantity of essential oil used in a recipe. This does not increase the benefit. Some oils can make you feel nauseous if used in excess, others are toxic. All are so powerful that they are measured in drops. Follow recipes carefully and exactly.

The two ways to dilute essential oils

❊ **By adding to water** This method is used for baths, inhalations, and room sprays. Drops are simply added to the poured out water immediately before use.

❊ **By adding to a plain carrier oil** This method is used for beauty treatments, massages and body moisturizers. (*See right for mixing.*)

CARRIER OILS

It is important to use pure, good quality cold-pressed vegetable oils as carriers for essential oils. These oils not only dilute essential oils so that they are safe, they also help to spread them evenly, slow down their evaporation rate and increase their absorption into the skin. Some carrier oils are suitable for use on the body, see page 39, some are specially good for the face, see page 29, and others are ideal for treating skin problems, see page 39.

How to blend essential oils with carrier oils

✳ **For immediate use**
1 Measure out the carrier oil into a glass measure.

2 Add the drops of essential oil and mix well.

✳ **To store for repeated use**
1 Measure the carrier oil into a dark-tinted glass bottle.

2 Add the drops of essential oil, mix well. Secure top.

✳ 3 Label the bottle clearly with the proportions of carrier oil to essential oil drops in the mix.

✳ **Use these basic proportions to mix essential oils with carrier oils for massage.** If you require different quantities to those shown simply increase or decrease in proportion.
15-20 drops essential oil in 60ml (2fl oz/ 12 tsp) carrier oil
7-10 drops essential oil in 30ml (1fl oz/ 6 tsp) carrier oil
3-5 drops essential oil in 15ml (½fl oz/ 12 tsp) carrier oil

BLEND SMALL AMOUNTS FOR BEST RESULTS

Blend oils for aromatherapy in small amounts so that they are as fresh and potent as possible when used.

Combining Oils

It is not difficult to create your own essential oil recipes but the golden rule is to keep mixes simple until you have had some practice. Some oils cancel the value of each other out, some clash, while other combinations can increase the therapeutic properties. See A-Z for relief of common health problems, pages 52-62, for some examples of possible therapeutic combinations.

TEN BEST OILS FOR MIXING

BERGAMOT • CHAMOMILE • FRANKINCENSE • GERANIUM • JASMINE
LAVENDER • NEROLI • ROSE • SANDALWOOD • YLANG-YLANG

TIPS ON COMBINING OILS

❋ Use no more than three essential oils in a mix, or four from one group (do not combine citrus oils), see page 21 for information on groups.

❋ Lavender and Rose mix with all other essential oils.

❋ Test out a combination before using (*see right*).

HOW TO TEST COMBINATIONS

1 Cut blotting paper into thin strips about 20cm (8in) in length.

2 Apply one drop of each oil to be used to the top of a different blotting paper strip. If one oil is to dominate apply two drops of the dominant oil.

3 Hold the strips together at the bottom to form a fan shape. Fan the oily tips backwards and forward under your nose and inhale. If you like the combination, go ahead and mix the oils.

Measuring out essential oils

- Most essential oil bottles have droppers built into the caps. When using an oil without a dropper use an eye-dropper or pipette to measure out droplets.
- Measure drops out quickly and accurately. Essential oils are volatile and evaporate rapidly.
- Wash the dropper thoroughly between uses if you are using the same dropper for more than one oil. The aroma will be ruined if you do not do this.

CHECK OIL COMBINATIONS ON RECIPIENT

If you are mixing the oils to use on someone else, do the test described above on them before you go ahead.

Storing Oils

Both undiluted and mixed oils need storing carefully if they are to remain in good condition.

UNDILUTED ESSENTIAL OILS

If you follow these three pointers your undiluted essential oils should keep in perfect condition for up to a year:

Store essential oils in a cool place • Store in dark glass, airtight bottles Store out of direct sunlight.

ESSENTIAL OILS DILUTED WITH A CARRIER OIL

These will keep for up to six months if you add the contents of a Vitamin E capsule, or one teaspoon of Wheatgerm oil. Either of these additions acts as an anti-oxidant and will help to preserve your mixture.

ALTERNATIVE STORAGE

Keep oils in the refrigerator to stop them going rancid.

Equipment Needed

❉ Glass measuring funnel which takes up to 100ml (4fl oz/½ cup) and shows teaspoon and tablespoon measures, plus a glass or plastic spoon for mixing.

❉ Ceramic (not metal) bowl for holding mixed oils while working.

❉ Small dark glass bottles with stoppered caps for storing pure essential oils, 10ml (½fl oz) size is ideal, plus similar larger bottles for storing combinations of essential and carrier oils.

❉ 4 eye-droppers/pipettes (you can manage with one but it will need washing thoroughly after each use).

❉ Small funnel for pouring carrier oils into bottles.

❉ Strips of blotting paper to test out mixes.

WARNING
Store both undiluted and diluted oils out of the reach of children

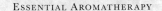

— 3 —
Beauty Treatments

Y ou can use essential oils to make your own beauty products.
This means that you can pick the best possible essential oils for
your particular skin. Since essential oils are so fine and have a
natural affinity with skin, they penetrate better than many
ingredients found in commercially available face creams and the
recipes are simple to produce and relatively cheap. As recipes
contain no preservatives, mix only enough of a recipe
to last for a few days and store in airtight, dark glass bottles.
Shake well before application.

BEST AROMATIC OILS FOR THE FACE

GERANIUM • JASMINE • LAVENDER • NEROLI • ROSE
VIOLET • YLANG-YLANG

BEST THERAPEUTIC OILS FOR THE FACE

Rashes and itchiness CHAMOMILE • Acne and oiliness JUNIPER
Open pores LEMONGRASS • Scars and slack skin MANDARIN
Sensitive skin MARIGOLD • Wrinkles ORANGE

BEST CARRIER OILS FOR THE FACE

Normal/combination skin SWEET ALMOND
Mature skin WHEATGERM • Sensitive skin PEACH KERNEL
Dry skin APRICOT KERNEL • Greasy/irritated skin JOJOBA

FOR CLEANSING

❋ **If you wash with soap and water** add 2 drops of essential oil to warm water for the final rinse. Stir to disperse, then pat the water on your face. Leave to air-dry instead of using a towel. The oil creates a film, protecting the skin.

❋ **If you use a light, oil-based lotion** replace this with 3 drops of essential oil added to 30ml (1fl oz/6 tsp) of SWEET ALMOND oil. Store in a dark glass bottle and shake well before pouring into your hand. Massage into the skin with your fingertips. Wipe off with damp cotton wool.

FOR MOISTURIZING

❋ Apply moisturizer morning and night to a well-cleansed skin. Put it on sparingly and massage in, smoothing gently.

FACIAL MOISTURIZER RECIPE

5 drops essential oil in 30ml (1fl oz/6 tsp) carrier oil, plus 1 tsp
Wheatgerm oil OR the contents of a Vitamin E capsule.

FACE MASKS

A moisturizing or deep-cleansing face mask improves your complexion. However a mask should not be used more than once a week. If used too often it can overstimulate the skin, making it drier or oilier. Apply your mask at night, as you need to lie back and rest while the mask does its work.

Mixing your own essential-oil face pack takes only a few minutes and uses simple ingredients, most of which you probably already have. Make enough each time for a single application and try different combinations of oils. Mix and use mask recipes within an hour. They will not keep.

Apply a mask to a well-cleansed skin by smoothing it on evenly in upward strokes. Avoid areas around eyes, nostrils and lips but apply to the neck. Relax for 10-15 minutes until the mask has dried. Rinse a moisturizing mask off with warm water. For a deep-cleansing facial use your fingertips to rub the dried mask away so you exfoliate the skin. Wash off any residue.

FACE MASK RECIPES

MOISTURIZING MASK

2 drops each Frankincense, Rose and Neroli in 30ml (1fl oz/6 tsp) Apricot oil with 5ml (⅙fl oz/1 tsp) warmed, clear honey, mixed with enough finely ground almond to make a soft paste.

DEEP-CLEANSING MASK

2 drops Geranium, 3 drops Lavender and 1 drop Lemon in 30ml (1fl oz/6 tsp) hot water, mixed with enough kaolin to make a smooth paste.

BODY MOISTURIZERS

An essential oil body treatment combines pure oil for maximum moisturization with the right therapeutic drops added for your needs. And that is all it is. You can use these moisturizers as much as you like; they are additive-free, pure, non-irritating, inexpensive, quick and easy to make.

The best time to apply a body moisturizer is after a bath or shower when skin is soft, warm, damp and slightly swollen with water. Alternatively rub the oil in using firm, rhythmic palm strokes to create maximum heat and friction. Mix just enough oil to last for a few days and apply it sparingly. The ideal body moisturizer recipe should have 15 drops of essential oil in 60ml (2fl oz / 12 teaspoons) carrier oil.

BODY MOISTURIZER RECIPES

RICH MOISTURIZERS

For dry skin 8 drops Myrrh, 7 drops Rose in 60ml (2fl oz / 12 tsp) Peanut oil.
For mature skin 7 drops Rose, 4 drops each Lavender and Sandalwood in 60ml (2fl oz / 12 tsp) Apricot Kernel oil.

LIGHT MOISTURIZERS

For oily skin 8 drops Lavender, 3 drops each Lemon and Petitgrain in 60ml (2fl oz / 12 tsp) Sunflower oil.
For itchy or sensitive skin 5 drops Rose, 9 drops Chamomile in 60ml (2fl oz / 12 tsp) Sweet Almond oil.

In the Bath

Relaxing in a warm, steamy bath with added essential oils is the most relaxing aromatherapy treatment possible. In this atmosphere the oils release even more aroma molecules than during massage, and as you lie soaking in the hot water the atmosphere softens skin and speeds up oil absorption, allowing the essential oils to work their magic more potently on both mind and body.
If you use more than one oil you will notice that you can smell both the whole bouquet and the blooms individually. Heat makes the smells of the individual oils come in waves, sometimes singly, sometimes together.
You can use essential oils in the bath to give almost any effect.
Depending on which oils you use, they can energize, relax, soothe, relieve aches and treat a cold, hangover or headache.

BATHTIME INGREDIENTS

❋ Warm room, neck pillow or rolled towel, soothing eye pads, warm towels.

❋ Introduce essential oils with the bathroom door shut and taps turned off.

❋ Add 8-10 drops maximum of essential oil for one bath, but use only 5 drops of stronger-smelling oils such as Eucalyptus, Lime, Rosemary and not more than 2- 3 drops Lemon.

❋ Add oils gently, drop by drop and leave to float on the water surface. In this way they coat your skin and mix as you step into the tub.

❋ Don't add extra oil when you are no longer aware of the scent. Oils keep evaporating for 15 minutes or more and small amounts often have greater effect than larger quantities which can irritate your skin.

BATHTIME RECIPES

RELAXING BATHS

In summer 4 drops Lavender, 4 drops Neroli, 2 drops Geranium.
In winter 3 drops Sandalwood, 3 drops Ylang-ylang, 2 drops Pine.
After a hard day 5 drops Rose, 5 drops Lavender.

INVIGORATING BATHS

In summer 2 drops Lemon, 3 drops Peppermint, 3 drops Rosemary.
In winter 3 drops Eucalyptus, 3 drops Clary Sage, 2 drops Peppermint.
After a hard day 5 drops Patchouli, 4 drops Peppermint.

Room Fresheners

Warming oil causes evaporation, adding the oil's subtle scent to a room. Essential oils can be introduced into a room to scent the air in a number of ways. A single essential oil scents a room best but remember you can ring the changes by using a different oil whenever you want.

WAYS TO INTRODUCE FRAGRANCE

❀ **Special burners** These are available with a saucer or bowl fixed above a stand which holds a candle or night light. Fill the saucer with hot water, add up to 8 drops of essential oil and light the candle beneath. This keeps the water hot enough for the oil to evaporate and scent the room. Alternatively drop oil in a saucer of hot water standing on a shelf above a central-heating radiator.

❀ **Scented light bulb rings** Made of compressed card, these rings sit around the neck of a light bulb. Add 4-5 drops of essential oil to the ring and as it heats the scent will be given off.

❀ **On a wood fire** Sprinkle a maximum of 12 drops of oil on three pieces of wood about 15 minutes before lighting a fire.

By spray Oil can be added to water in a pump-action houseplant spray bottle. Add 10 drops of essential oil to half a litre (1 pint/2½ cups) of water, shake well then pump four or five sprays into the air to deodorize, freshen and scent the room.

In pot pourri Make your own pot pourri by drying leaves, flowers and herbs from your garden. Add spices, talcum powder and a favourite essential oil. To six cups of dried plant material add two tablespoons of talc and 12 drops of essential oil. Leave the mix in an airtight container, gently shaking and inverting the container daily for a couple of weeks until the aromas have been absorbed by the talc and dried materials. Then place the pot pourri in an open bowl to give off the fragrance.

SOME SUGGESTED POT POURRI INGREDIENTS

Flowers	Aromatic leaves	Spices and citrus peel
Scented roses	Chamomile	Cinnamon
Lavender	Cotton Lavender	Nutmeg
Lilac	Sweet Basil	Mace
Mimosa	Lemon Thyme	Cloves
Jasmine	Bay	Allspice
Honeysuckle	Tarragon	Orange and Lemon Peel

Household Cleansers

M any essential oils have powerful disinfectant properties
that kill germs and improve hygiene and they do not need the addition of
environmentally damaging chemicals to help them clean effectively.

BEST OIL MIXES FOR CLEANSING

Kitchen surfaces LEMON and GERANIUM • Toilets TEA TREE
or PINE • Baths, basins, sinks LEMON and LAVENDER •
Washing up GERANIUM and LAVENDER

CLEANSER RECIPES

KITCHEN CLEANSER

For surfaces, chopping boards and floors add 8 drops of essential oil to a small bucket
of warm water. Use on a damp cloth or floor sponge.

BATHROOM CLEANSER

To clean basins, toilets, baths and sinks use a damp cloth to which 3 drops of
essential oil have been added.

DISHES AND CUTLERY RINSE

Add 2 drops of essential oil to the rinsing water after washing up.

Insect Repellents

Essential oils make excellent natural, fragrant,
non-toxic insecticides which are kind to humans but repulsive to insects.

BEST INSECT REPELLENT OILS

For moths CAMPHOR.

For mosquitoes CITRONELLA. A few drops of oil on your pillowcase or mattress should drive away droning mosquitoes. To help to keep them away and soothe the itchiness of insect bites dilute 6 drops of essential oil in 30ml (1fl oz/6 tsp) Sunflower oil and rub this into any exposed skin before going to bed.

For most flying insects LEMONGRASS. Mix 15 drops of essential oil with 600ml (20fl oz/1pint) water in a pump action spray bottle, shake well, then use to spray flying insects.

For ants, fleas and most insects TEA TREE and THYME. Dilute 8 drops of Tea Tree and 7 drops of Thyme in 30ml (1fl oz/6 tsp) water in a spray bottle and spray areas where ants or cockroaches walk.

For pet fleas dilute 6 drops of GERANIUM, 5 drops of LAVENDER, 4 drops of TEA TREE in 30ml (1fl oz/6 tsp) of water in a spray bottle. Spray into brushed up fur, avoiding the animal's eyes.

— 4 —
First steps in Massage

Peace, quiet and a warm room are important for massage as they not only relax the recipient but warmth brings out the aromas of the oils used. Make sure your hands are warm and have lots of large, warm towels available to act as pillows and padding. Prepare a side table with everything you will need. Mix up just enough massage oil and place it in a bowl big enough to dip your fingers in, or in a plastic bottle with a squirting top. Warm the oil by standing the container in hot water. Aromatherapy massage is made up of six basic movements which are shown on pages 40-45.

TIPS FOR A SUCCESSFUL MASSAGE

❋ Try a massage out on yourself. Soothing foot massage and anti-wrinkle massage can both be done as self massages.

❋ Apply enough oil to make your hands slip but not slide. First spread a small amount of warm oil onto the skin with smooth, flowing rhythmic strokes. Add more to your hands when they start to drag over the skin.

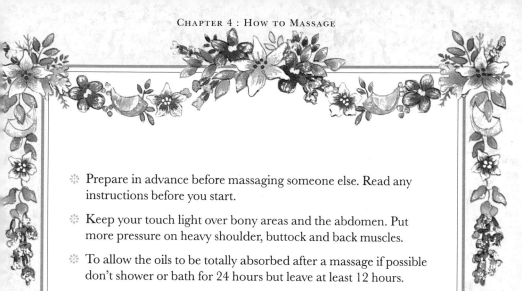

* Prepare in advance before massaging someone else. Read any instructions before you start.

* Keep your touch light over bony areas and the abdomen. Put more pressure on heavy shoulder, buttock and back muscles.

* To allow the oils to be totally absorbed after a massage if possible don't shower or bath for 24 hours but leave at least 12 hours.

BEST SINGLE ESSENTIAL OILS FOR MASSAGE

BERGAMOT • GERANIUM • LAVENDER • NEROLI • ORANGE
ROSE • YLANG-YLANG

Insomnia, tension CHAMOMILE • Colds EUCALYPTUS
Invigorating PEPPERMINT • Headaches ROSEMARY
PMT, depression CLARY SAGE • Sedative SANDALWOOD

BEST CARRIER OILS FOR THE BODY

GRAPESEED • SWEET ALMOND • SUNFLOWER • SAFFLOWER
PEANUT • SOYA • SESAME

BEST CARRIER OILS FOR SKIN PROBLEMS

Scars WHEAT GERM • Stretch marks SESAME
Wrinkles APRICOT KERNEL or EVENING PRIMROSE • Oily skin
SAFFLOWER or SUNFLOWER • Normal, itchy or sensitive skin
SWEET ALMOND • Dry skin PEANUT • Rough skin OLIVE OIL

BASIC MASSAGE MOVEMENT 1

Stroking

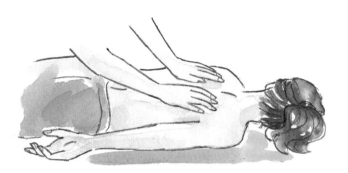

This is the simplest massage movement and is done with both palms down and hands flat. You may do it with one hand following the other, a if you were stroking a cat. Alternatively place hands parallel and move them in unison in the same direction.

BASIC MASSAGE MOVEMENT 2

Raking

·

Pretend your fingertips are the ends of a rake. Keeping them bent but stiff at the joints, and with fingertips touching the skin, make firm, pulling movements back towards you. In this movement, you may choose to use both hands together, or one following the other in a repeated action.

BASIC MASSAGE MOVEMENT 3

Pummelling

Make your hands into fists. Keep fingers relaxed and bounce fists one after the other in a fast drumming movement up and down on the body. You can pummel with your fingertips towards the body, or, as shown, sideways with your thumbs uppermost and little fingers down. You can also use the back of your hands with palms turned upwards.

BASIC MASSAGE MOVEMENT 4

Friction Rub

With palms down and hands flat, move one forward while
the other moves backward in a short, fast sawing movement
along or across the body.

BASIC MASSAGE MOVEMENT 5

Kneading

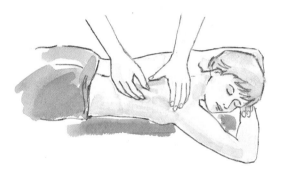

Place your hands flat on the body with fingers together and thumbs at right angles. Then use your thumbs to push and pinch flesh up towards the fingers. Move them one after the other over the same area of flesh.

BASIC MASSAGE MOVEMENT 6

Thumbing

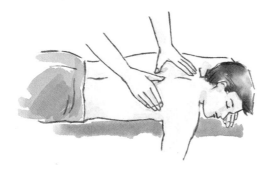

Use the pad and side of your thumb to knead into the flesh, stroking deeply. You can also make small, deep circles with the thumb tips. Over deep muscle tissue use them to press down, hold, then release.

Back Massage

The large, smooth space of the back makes this an ideal place to learn the strokes. It is also a tangle of muscles and nerves and responds dramatically to the right touch. Lay the recipient down on a well-padded floor or a firm mattress with a small pillow under the upper chest so the head and neck are relaxed in the face down position. For a body massage use 15 drops essential oil in 60ml (2fl oz/12 tsp) carrier oil. For a back massage only use 5 drops essential oil in 15ml (½fl oz/3 tsp) carrier oil.

BEST OILS FOR BACK MASSAGE

BERGAMOT • LAVENDER • EUCALYPTUS • ORANGE
FRANKINCENSE • PETITGRAIN

1 **Stroking** Place hands about 5 cm (2in) from spine on either side of the lower back. Slide them up to the top of the back, over the shoulders and down again. Use a heavier movement for the upwards stroke. Do this for several minutes.

2 **Stroking** Place your hands, palms down, halfway up the spine and slide them apart sideways so that one ends up at the base of the spine, the other between the shoulder blades. Repeat diagonally in first one, then the opposite direction, making long, firm strokes. Hold skin taught at the end for a few seconds, then release.

3 **Friction rub** Repeat step 1 but this time slide your hands over the shoulders and down to the collar bones. Place your hands under one hip, fingers down, and pull upwards from the side of the body towards the spine, using one hand after the other in a continuous movement. Work up one side of the body, across the top of the shoulders and down the other side to the opposite hip.

4 **Kneading** Repeat step 1 from waist to neck then do smaller circles, using fingertip pressure, around and over each shoulder blade. Knead the upper back and sides of the neck then repeat a few strokes from Step 1.

5 **Thumbing** Place one thumb either side of the spine, 3cm (1in) out on either side of lower back. Press thumb pads down for a count of five then relax to relax the spinal support muscles. Repeat, moving up the back towards the neck. Then repeat from lower back to neck, making tiny circles with each thumb. Run your fingers firmly up and down the area then repeat Step 1.

6 **Raking** Make circular movements with the fingertips from the base of back up to the neck. Use the raking movements starting at the neck and working down to the hips, one hand following the other. Finish raking with light, slow movements.

Soothing Foot Massage

Nothing is better for tired feet than a foot soak and aromatherapy massage. This is guaranteed to put the spring back into your step. Sit in an upright chair then, after massaging each foot, stretch out flat for ten minutes with your feet propped higher than your head. Use 5 drops of essential oil in 15ml (½fl oz/3 tsp) carrier oil.

BEST OILS FOR FOOT MASSAGE

CITRONELLA • GERANIUM • LAVENDER • LEMON
PEPPERMINT • ROSEMARY

1 **Soaking** Place a large bowl of hot water on the floor in front of your chair, and surrounded by towels. Soak both feet for 10 minutes then start the massage on one foot, while still wet.

2 **Friction rub** Leave one foot in the bowl. Cross the other leg so that the calf of this leg rests on the thigh of the first leg. Sandwich your foot between your hands and do a fast friction rub. Start with one hand on the instep, the other on the top of the foot. Repeat on toes and instep. Then place palms on either side of the ankle and repeat, massaging briskly.

3 **Stretching** Do a series of foot stretches to loosen tendons. Hold each stretch for a count of ten. Point your toes and flex them, hold, push down, hold. Turn your foot to the left, hold, to the right, hold, then, still pointing your toes, make large slow circles to rotate the ankle. Place your hands palm down over the toes with the fingers wrapped over the sole. Keep your foot at 90 degrees to the leg and push the toes down to flex and stretch them. Hold. Then gently pull upwards and hold.

4 **Thumbing** Use the tips of your thumb and index finger to make quick pinches all over the heel of the foot. Then wrap your fingers around the top of the foot with thumbs across the sole, under the arch. Do deep, flowing thumb strokes one after the other from heel to instep along the arch of the foot. Follow by using the thumbs to make small circles all over the sole in a light, kneading movement.

5 **Thumbing and friction rub** Firmly rub each toe from base to tip between your thumb (on top) and index finger (below). Then do several deep thumb-strokes up the underside of each toe by wrapping your fingers across the tops of toes, bending your thumb underneath, and using it to do the firm, slow, pushing-in movement. Finish with a fast friction rub over the toes to warm them and increase blood circulation.

6 **Kneading** Use your thumb to knead and rub all around the ankle bone then, using your index finger and thumb, pinch all the way up the tendon at the back of the heel. Repeat foot stretches in Step 3 but this time keep both hands wrapped around your ankle as you point, flex and circle feet. Finish with several full foot strokes. Place one hand on top of the foot, palm down and the other under the foot, palm up. Start at the toes and, with hands working in unison, do a firm, slow pull with hands following the contours of the foot back up to the ankle.

Anti-wrinkle Massage

Although wrinkles may be a sign of a life well-lived, none of us like to see them appearing. The best way to postpone wrinkles is to protect the skin from sun and to make sure that it is well moisturized. Massage using 5 drops of essential oil in 15ml (½fl oz/3 tsp) carrier oil.

BEST OILS FOR ANTI-WRINKLE FACE MASSAGE

GERANIUM • LAVENDER • MYRRH • NEROLI • ORANGE • ROSE

1 **Forehead** Stretch your neck by bending your head back and holding for a count of six while you open your eyes wide and raise your eyebrows. With head upright, place your index fingers next to one another on the bridge of the nose and stroke upwards, one after the other from brow to forehead. Every sixth stroke take one finger out firmly along each brow and press into the temple for a count of three. Repeat several times. Then, using the flat of your hand, palm-stroke up the forehead.

2 **Eyes** Place each index finger at the outer eye corner, then move them gradually along the under eye, making gentle inward presses for a count of three until you reach the tear ducts. Use very light pressure. Repeat along the top eyelids on the browbone. Don't stretch or drag, rather press in, lift, then press again. Place the heel of each hand over each eye and gently press. Count to 20. Finally screw your eyes tightly closed and hold for a count of five. Then open them wide and roll the eyes in slow circles three times in each direction.

3 **Jawline** Stretch the neck by bending the head to one side, hold for a count of ten, then repeat on the other side. Hold your head straight, use the backs of the fingertips to stroke from collarbone up to chin in a rhythmic, flowing movement. Then, with palms facing upwards, use the first three fingertips of each hand to do a light, outward flick under the chin, in a rapid drumming motion across the jawline from ear to ear. With thumbs and index fingers, lightly pinch along the jawbone from chin out to earlobes. Repeat back to the middle of the chin.

4 **Mouth** Open your mouth wide and with a relaxed jaw, move your chin to the left, hold for a count of five then repeat to the right. Place the tips of your little fingers on the middle of your bottom lip, press in, hold for a count of five, then repeat, gradually moving out to the corners of the mouth, then up and over the top lip to the centre of the nose. Repeat as a light stroke.

5 **Cheeks** Place the palms of your hands against the sides of your face and stroke with a fast, light touch in an upwards direction to stimulate circulation and bring the colour to your cheeks. Repeat strokes using a flowing, firm stretch upwards. Finish by pressing the palms of your hands over your face and holding for a count of 20.

— 5 —

A–Z for relief of common health problems

The anti-bacterial and antiseptic properties of essential oils make them excellent for use to provide relief for many minor health problems. Do *not* apply essential oils undiluted unless specifically mentioned here. Turn to Chapter 2, pages 20-27 on how to use and dilute oils and Chapter 3, pages 28-37 on alternative methods of application. When mixing the essential oils recommended here with carrier oil use the basic proportions shown on page 23 and massage gently into the affected area. When using essential oils for relief in the bath, follow the recommended quantities on page 33. Do check all these guidleines before launching into your treatment: essential oils must be used in the right way as some can be toxic if misused. If symptoms persist call a doctor.

ACNE

Acne and skin eruptions are caused by the over-production of oil in the sebaceous glands. Many essential oils have a soothing and healing effect on problem skin. They also soothe the mental stresses that can make acne worse.

Oils to use

Antiseptic, healing and oil regulators BERGAMOT, CEDARWOOD, GERANIUM, JUNIPER, LAVENDER, LEMON, ROSEWOOD, SANDALWOOD, TEA TREE, YARROW
Boils or inflammation CHAMOMILE, PETITGRAIN
Cleansing LEMONGRASS, PATCHOULI

ATHLETE'S FOOT

This is a fungal infection of the feet. Skin between the toes becomes red and itchy and peels. Athlete's foot is very contagious and is easily caught from wet floors of communal changing-rooms and showers, where the fungus thrives.

Oils to use

Antiseptic, healing LAVENDER • Anti-fungal TEA TREE
Anti-inflammatory, soothing BIRCH, GERANIUM
Deodorizing, drying LEMONGRASS

WARNING

If you are pregnant check the list of essential oils to be avoided on page 9. Consult your doctor before using aromatherapy to treat any condition.

BACKACHE

Backache and muscular pain affect almost everyone at some point in their lives. They may be caused by lifting heavy weights, bad posture, too much or too little exercise, a fall, pregnancy, or even a powerful sneeze.

Oils to use

Relaxing, warming BAY, CAMPHOR, CITRONELLA, EUCALYPTUS, MARJORAM, PINE, SPRUCE

Soothing, stimulating AMBRETTE, JUNIPER, PETITGRAIN, ROSEMARY

Anti-inflammatory, relaxes muscles CLARY SAGE, LAVENDER, THYME.

BITES AND STINGS

Insect bites and stings respond well to essential oils. Those oils that are antiseptic and anti-inflammatory help reduce swelling, itchiness and inflammation.

Oils to use

Anti-inflammatory, antiseptic, soothing BASIL, CHAMOMILE, CITRONELLA, LAVENDER, MARIGOLD, PEPPERMINT, TEA TREE

BRUISES

A bruise shows that tissue has been injured, usually by a bump or knock. The purple, black or yellow discolouration, which remains long after the initial pain has gone, is due to blood seepage from damaged capillaries.

Oils to use

Increase circulation, warming CAMPHOR, CLARY SAGE

Soothing CALENDULA, GERANIUM, MARJORAM

Anti-inflammatory CYPRESS, LAVENDER

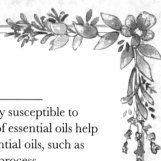

MINOR BURNS

The blisters and inflammation of burnt skin are very susceptible to infection. The anti-bacterial and antiseptic properties of essential oils help protect the area while new skin grows and some essential oils, such as lavender, help speed up the natural healing process.

See also SUNBURN.

Oils to use
Antiseptic, healing, soothing LAVENDER, TEA TREE (both can be applied undiluted to burnt skin immediately)
Healing, soothing CHAMOMILE, GERANIUM, MARIGOLD, ROSE

CHILBLAINS

These appear as swollen, discoloured veins on the fingers, toes and the backs of legs after exposure to very cold weather.

Oils to use
Soothing, warming EUCALYPTUS, GINGER, SPRUCE
Circulation boosting CYPRESS, JUNIPER, LEMONGRASS, LEMON, MARJORAM, ROSEMARY, TEA TREE

COLDS

The common cold is so infectious it is almost inescapable during winter.
Caused by a wide range of ever-changing viruses, symptoms can include a
high temperature, aching, sore eyes, sore throat, coughing, sneezing and
chest and nose congestion. Essential oils can help soothe some of these
symptoms, but nothing known to science so far will cure a cold.

Oils to use

Decongestant EUCALYPTUS, LAVENDER, LEMON, LIME, MARJORAM,
PEPPERMINT, PINE, TEA TREE • Relieve sinus congestion ANGELICA, BAY,
CAMPHOR, MYRRH, SPRUCE, THYME • Strengthens resistance LAUREL

COUGHS

An irritating cough, caused by anything from dust and cigarette smoke to
the common cold, can drive anyone to distraction. Inhaled essential oils
are effective at soothing a cough, *see HEADACHE* for quantities.

Oils to use

Expectorant ANGELICA, ATLAS CEDARWOOD, EUCALYPTUS, MYRRH,
PEPPERMINT, SANDALWOOD, SPRUCE, THYME
Calming, relaxing FRANKINCENSE • Decongestant GINGER, ROSEMARY

CRAMP

The excruciating, involuntary muscle spasm known as cramp can be
caused by the onset of menstruation, poor circulation, too much exercise
or a vitamin deficiency. Cramp usually hits hardest at night.
Essential oils help to warm and relax the tense muscles,
ease the pain and, if need be, put you back to sleep.

Oils to use

Warming and relaxing EUCALYPTUS, LEMON, MANDARIN, MARJORAM
Boosts circulation JUNIPER • For period cramp FENNEL, JASMINE,
LAUREL, TARRAGON • Relaxing, soporific AMBRETTE SEED,
CHAMOMILE, LAVENDER, NEROLI, ROSE, YLANG-YLANG

MINOR CUTS AND ABRASIONS

Essential oils are excellent at soothing, disinfecting and healing minor
cuts and skin abrasions from nappy rash to shaving nicks.

Oils to use

Anti-bacterial, antiseptic BERGAMOT, CHAMOMILE, CITRONELLA,
LAVENDER, TEA TREE • Soothing, healing GERANIUM, MARIGOLD

DANDRUFF

This occurs when there is an imbalance of oils at the skin's surface and is
caused by overactive sebaceous glands. It comes in two forms: fine, dry
flakes on the scalp, or sticky, oily scales. Both types are itchy.
Essential oils are excellent at treating dandruff
and can usually remove symptoms.

Oils to use

Anti-inflammatory, oil-regulating, antiseptic TEA TREE
Antiseptic, astringent BAY, BIRCH, CEDARWOOD, JUNIPER, LEMON,
ROSEMARY • Antiseptic, soothing GERANIUM, LAVENDER, SANDALWOOD

HANGOVER

The morning after too much alcohol often leaves us lethargic,
nauseous and with a headache.
Treat with an aromatherapy bath. Lie back with a neck pillow made
from an ice pack and drink plenty of water.

Oils to use
Soothing, uplifting GERANIUM, LAVENDER, NEROLI, ROSE.
Clears the head, energizes, reduces nausea LEMON, PEPPERMINT

HEADACHE

Tension, noise, lights, action and too much thinking can all
make headaches worse.
For relief inhale one of the essential oils shown below. Place 1 litre
(2 pints/5 cups) of boiling water in a heat retaining bowl, and add 5 drops
of essential oil to the surface of the water. Bend over the bowl and
drape a large towel over your head to trap the evaporating oils and steam.
Inhale the vapours for a few minutes, add a little more boiling
water to evaporate off any remaining oil,
then lie in a darkened room.

Oils to use
Clear the head EUCALYPTUS, LEMONGRASS, PEPPERMINT
Relaxing, analgesic AMBRETTE SEED, CHAMOMILE, LAVENDER, VIOLET
Relieve tension CLARY SAGE, FRANKINCENSE, THYME

INDIGESTION

Indigestion, heartburn and flatulence are usually the results of eating
too quickly or too much, eating a spicy, rich diet or
going for long periods without food.
Essential oils massaged into the stomach with slow, circular, clockwise
strokes can bring relief. Alternatively try inhaling the aromas from a
tissue. Use no more than 2 drops of oil and place the tissue under your
pillow at night or in a breast pocket or tucked into a bra during the day.

Oils to use

Digestives ANGELICA, FENNEL, LAVENDER, MARJORAM, PEPPERMINT,
TARRAGON • Warming, relaxing AMBRETTE SEED, MANDARIN

INFLUENZA

This is a more serious viral infection than the common cold and puts
most people in bed for a couple of days.
Essential oils can soothe some of the symptoms and help to prevent
the virus taking too firm a hold on the flu-ravaged body.

Oils to use

Clear head and congestion EUCALYPTUS, LIME, PEPPERMINT, ROSEMARY
Expectorants, decongestants MARJORAM, SPRUCE, THYME
Boost the immune system LAUREL, ORANGE

INSOMNIA

Not being able to sleep is deeply irritating, exhausting, and distressing
but worrying about it won't help.
Instead of lying there counting sheep have an aromatherapy bath.
Use oils with calming, sedative qualities.

Oils to use

Calming, sedative BASIL, CHAMOMILE, CYPRESS, GERANIUM, JASMINE,
LAVENDER, MANDARIN, MARJORAM, MIMOSA, NEROLI, PETITGRAIN,
ROSE, SANDALWOOD, VALERIAN, YARROW, YLANG-YLANG

JETLAG

This disorienting experience can result in your finding it difficult to sleep,
having swollen feet, dehydrated skin and possibly loss of appetite.
To help you adjust to time differences faster, use LAVENDER oil when you
land and want to stay awake, GERANIUM when you want to sleep.

Oils to use

Reviving LAVENDER • Relaxing, calming GERANIUM
For swelling CYPRESS • Head clearing PEPPERMINT

MENOPAUSE

This starts with the natural reduction of oestrogen and progesterone
hormones, signalling the end of the childbearing years. It can begin at any
time from around 40 to 60 years. While many women notice little change,
others suffer from a wide range of unpleasant symptoms from hot flushes
and lack of confidence to abdominal pain and deep depression.

Oils to use

Rebalancing CHAMOMILE, ROSE
Regulate hormone production CYPRESS, GERANIUM, LAVENDER
Anti-depressants CLARY SAGE, PEPPERMINT, YLANG-YLANG.

NAUSEA

The only thing worse than feeling sick is actually being sick.
Common triggers include a rich or spicy meal, contaminated food,
a rotten smell, stress, fear, the motion of travel or migraine.
A little essential oil inhaled from a tissue can help tremendously.
Use no more than 2 drops of oil and place the tissue under your pillow
at night or in a breast pocket or tucked into a bra during the day.

Oils to use

Settle the stomach GINGER, LEMON, MANDARIN, PEPPERMINT

SUNBURN

Now that we all know that sunbathing ages the skin and causes cancer
this is something that should no longer be a problem. However, if you do
burn, essential oils can boost the skin's natural healing process
and soothe and cool the initial burning.

Oils to use

Soothing, anti-inflammatory CHAMOMILE, GERANIUM, LAVENDER, ROSE

THRUSH, CANDIDA, FUNGAL PROBLEMS

The most useful essential oil for vaginal or genital fungal infections is Tea Tree. It has amazing anti-fungal and disinfectant properties that have only recently been recognized. It is also safe and non-irritating to sensitive genital tissue. Apply one part essential oil to 10 parts warm water and use to bathe the affected area or as a douche. Some other antiseptic oils can help to soothe, heal and reduce itchiness.

Oils to use
Anti-fungal TEA TREE
Antiseptic JUNIPER, LAVENDER, MYRRH, SANDALWOOD

TRAVEL SICKNESS

Usually caused by the motion of travelling by air, sea or land, the nausea can also be due to a fear of travelling.

Oils to use
Calming, settle the stomach GINGER, LEMON, MANDARIN, PEPPERMINT
Uplifting, soothing BERGAMOT

INDEX